Give yourself a star when you've finished an activity.

Use these stickers on the puzzle in the middle of the book.

10 Minutes a Day

Handwriting

for ages 5-7

This CGP book is bursting with quick
Handwriting activities for children aged 5-7.

Plus, it's packed with colourful stickers so they'll have
fun while they're learning all the essential skills!

Hints for Helpers

Here are a few things to bear in mind when using this book:

- The first half of the book covers letter formation, and the second half covers joined-up (cursive) writing.

- Every school has its own handwriting style. Some schools may form letters and joins differently to how they're written here. Check with your child's school to see how they write and join each letter.

- This book includes break letters, which aren't joined to other letters. Some schools have different break letters (for example, g can be a break letter or it can be joined up). Check which break letters your child's school uses.

- Throughout the book, the red dots show where to start writing. The first example of each letter or type of join also has arrows to follow.

- It's best to work through the book in order — it gets harder as you go through, and later pages build on content covered earlier. The 'Perfect pastimes' activity on p.30-31 includes content from the whole book, so you may want to save this activity until last.

- You can help by encouraging your child to sit up straight at a desk or table, and by helping them to hold their pencil correctly, using three fingers to manoeuvre it. This is called a 'tripod grip'.

- Encourage your child to work neatly, keeping their letters the same size. The guidelines will help with this — they show where each letter should sit, and where the top and bottom of each letter should be.

Published by CGP

Editors: Aimee Ashurst, Keith Blackhall, Catherine Heygate, Nathan Mair

With thanks to Kirsty Sweetman and Lucy Towle for the proofreading.

With thanks to Jan Greenway for the copyright research.

ISBN: 978 1 83774 020 8

Printed by Elanders Ltd, Newcastle upon Tyne.

Graphics used on the cover and throughout the book © Educlips 2023
Cover design concept by emc design ltd.

Text, design, layout and original illustrations
© Coordination Group Publications Ltd. (CGP) 2023
All rights reserved.

CGP, Broughton House, Griffin Street,
Broughton-in-Furness, Cumbria, LA20 6HH

CGP c/o Elanders GmbH, Anton-Schmidt-Str. 15,
71332 Waiblingen, GERMANY info@elanders-germany.com

Photocopying this book is not permitted, even if you have a CLA licence.
Extra copies are available from CGP with next day delivery • 0800 1712 712 • www.cgpbooks.co.uk

Contents

c, o and a 2

i, l and t 4

e, s and f 6

u, y and j 8

r and n 10

m and p 12

d, g and q 14

h, b and k 16

v, w, x and z 18

Capital letters 20

Numbers 22

A trip to the zoo 24

A recipe for pancakes 25

The Vikings 26

Jay's shop 27

Squid 28

Hibba the detective 29

Puzzle: Perfect pastimes 30

Joining to small letters
The first join 32

Joining to e 34

Joining small and tall letters
The second join 36

Joining to round letters
The third join 39

Joining to s 42

Joining from the top
The fourth join 43

Joining from f 46

More joining from the top
The fifth join 47

More joining from f 50

More joining to round letters
The sixth join 51

Break letters 54

The school assembly 57

The friendly monster 58

Ancient Egypt 59

Under construction 60

A trip to the post office 61

The potion 62

c, o and a

How It Works

Trace each letter. Then copy them. Start each letter at the red dot.

Now Try These

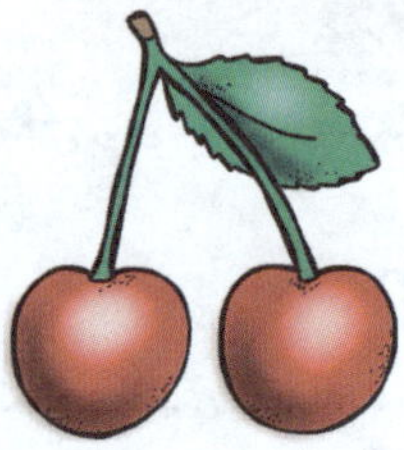

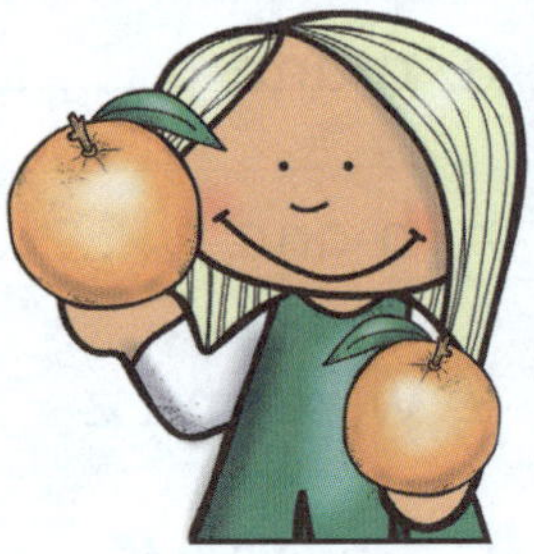

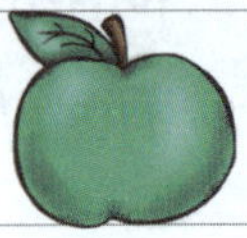

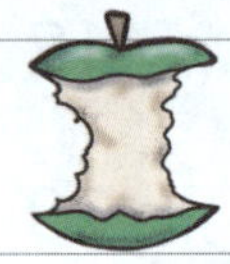

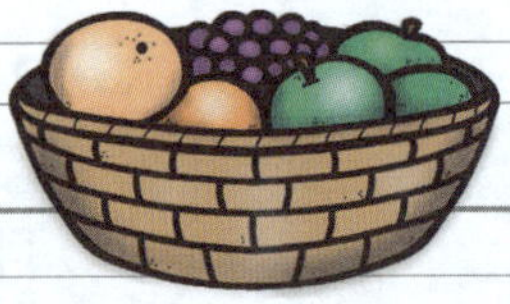

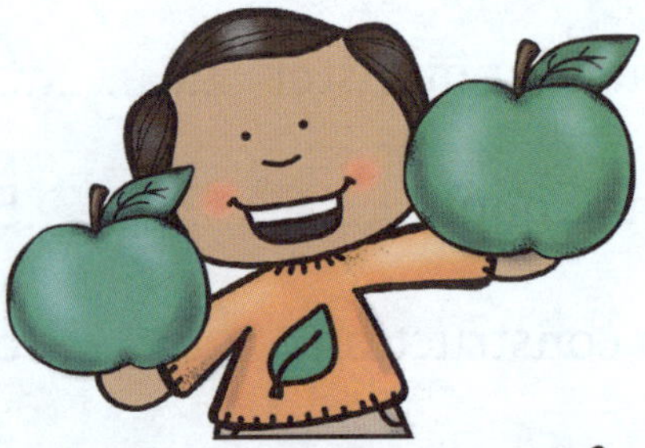

Cool! Give yourself a sticker.

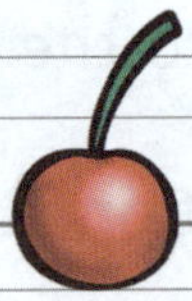

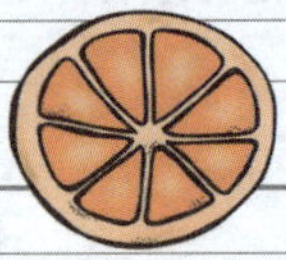

c, o and a

How It Works

Trace the letters to complete each word. Then copy them.

Now Try These

magic   m gi   m gi

cards   rds   rds

shock   sh k   sh k

 clap   l p   l p

cool   l   l

cloak   l k   l k

Wow! Make a sticker appear.

i, l and t

How It Works

Start at the red dot and trace each letter. Then copy them.

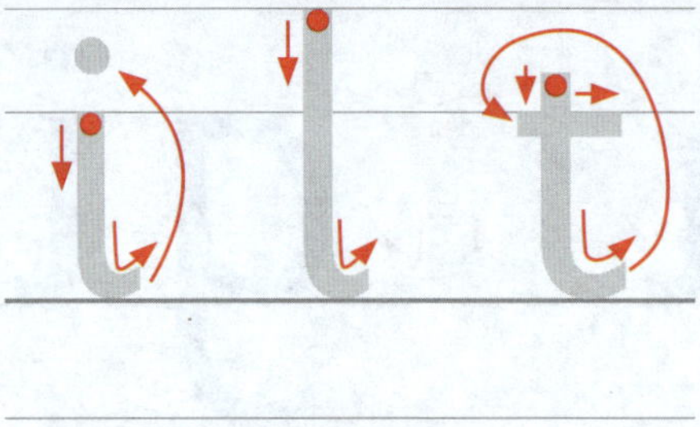

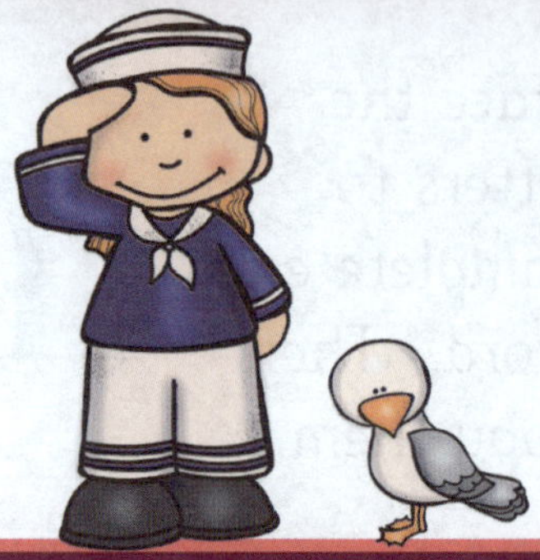

Now Try These

i i i

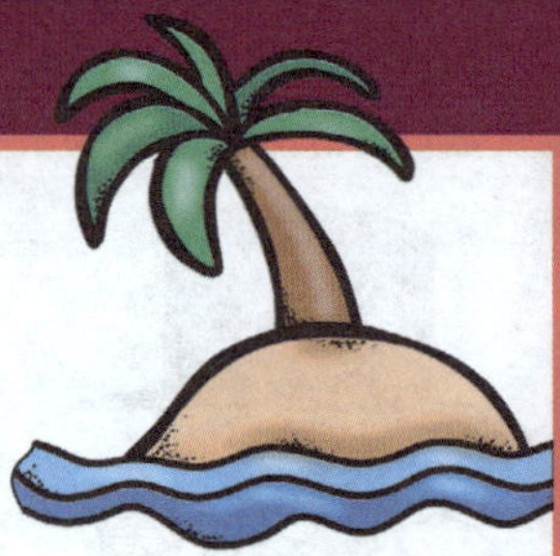

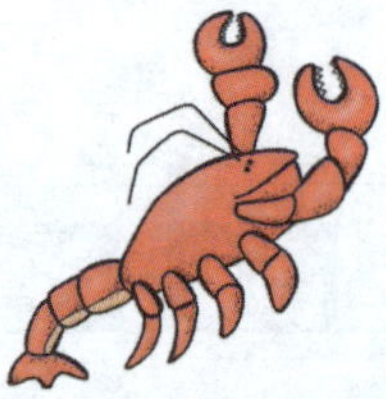

l l l

t t t

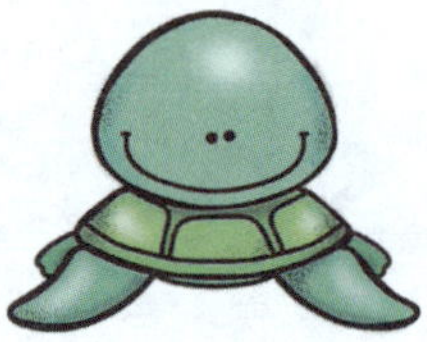

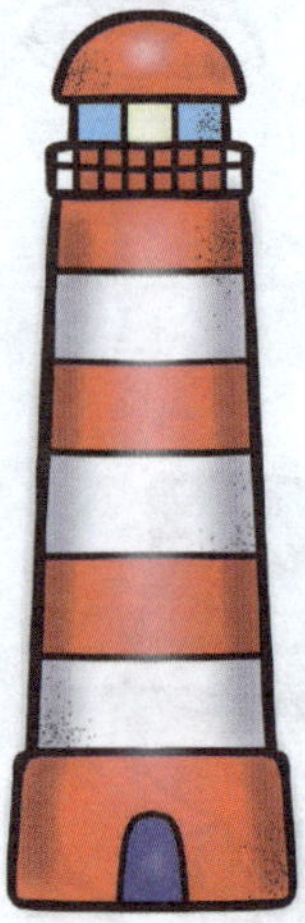

i i l l

t t

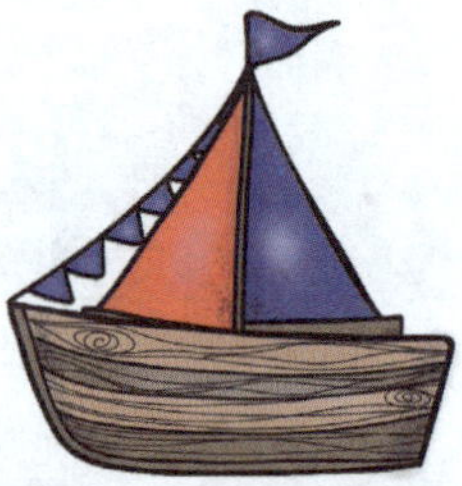

i 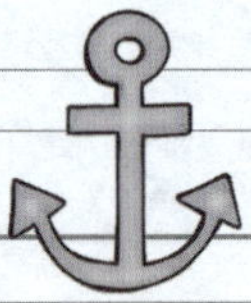 l 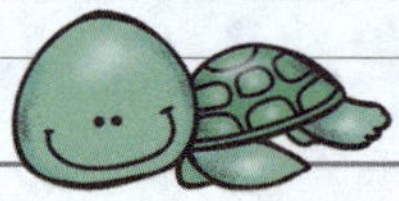 t

Incredible! Stick on a sticker.

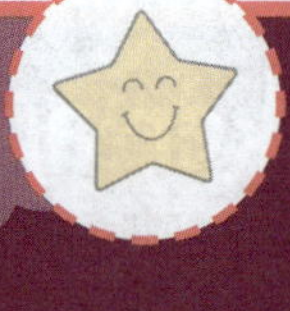

i, l and t

How It Works

Trace the letters to complete each word. Then copy them. Start each letter at the red dot.

Now Try These

cat

cute   ue   ue

bowl   b w   b w

kitten   k   en   k   en

little   e   e

collar   r   r

Pawfect! Take a sticker.

e, s and f

How It Works

Start at the red dot and trace each letter. Then copy them.

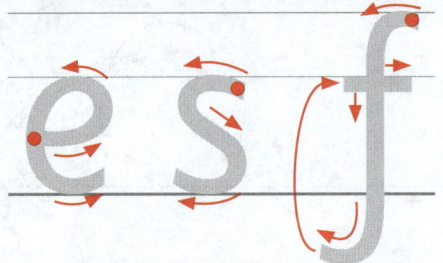

Now Try These

e e e

s s s

f f f

feast

salt

taste

Delicious! Get a sticker.

e, s and f

How It Works

Trace these words, then copy them. Start each letter at the red dot.

Now Try These

east

floats

sail fast  close cliffs

 see a fat seal

Ahoy! Go and find a sticker.

u, y and j

How It Works

Trace each letter. Then copy them. Start each letter at the red dot.

Now Try These

u u u

y y y

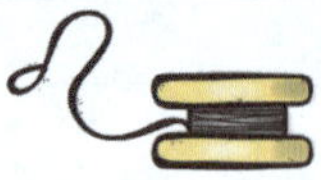

j j j

full

toys

jet

You are great! Pop on a sticker.

u, y and j

How It Works

Trace each of these words, starting at the red dot each time. Then copy them.

joy

Now Try These

joy

leafy

just so joyful

you feel jolly

Did you enjoy that? Take a sticker.

r and n

How It Works

Trace each letter and word, and then copy them. Remember to start at the red dot.

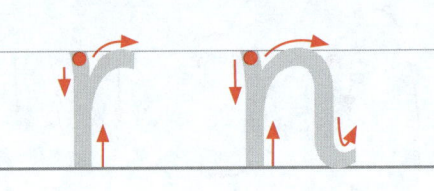

Now Try These

r r r

n n n

car

 tyre

train

 turn

You're on the road to success! Have a sticker.

r and n

How It Works

Trace each word.
Then copy them.
Remember to start
at the red dot.

rain

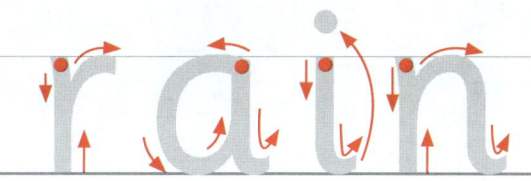

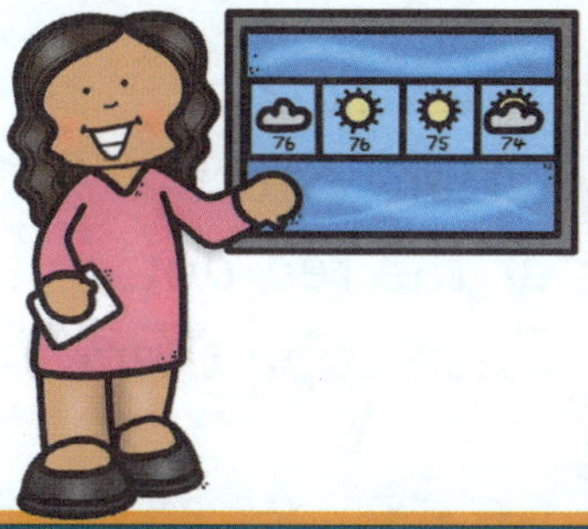

Now Try These

raincoat

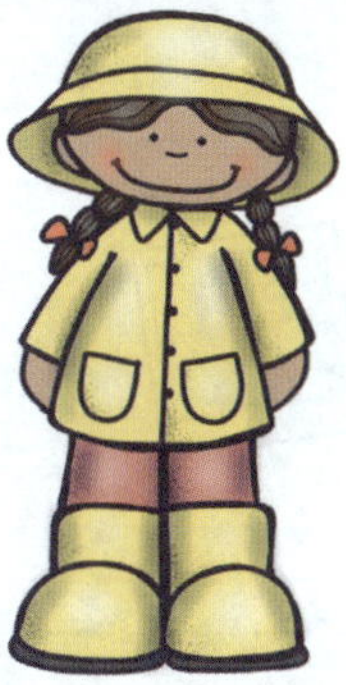

sunny

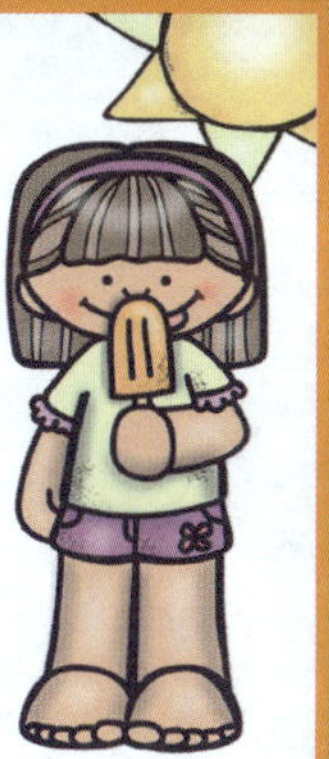

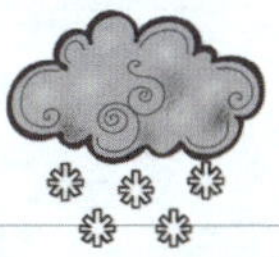

too frosty

carrot nose

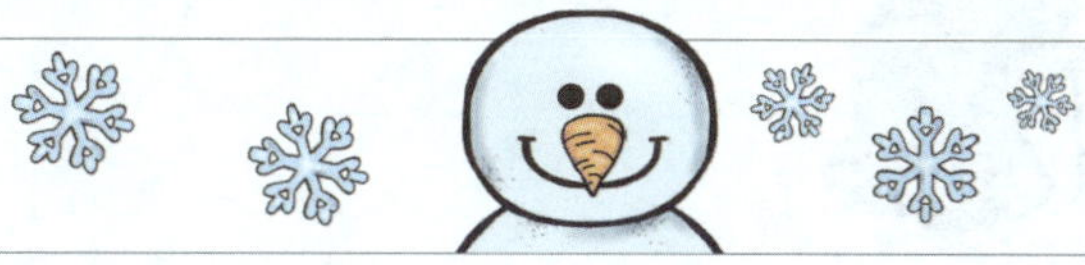

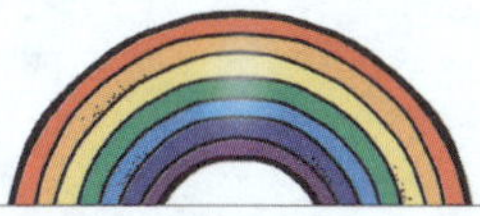

you can join our fun

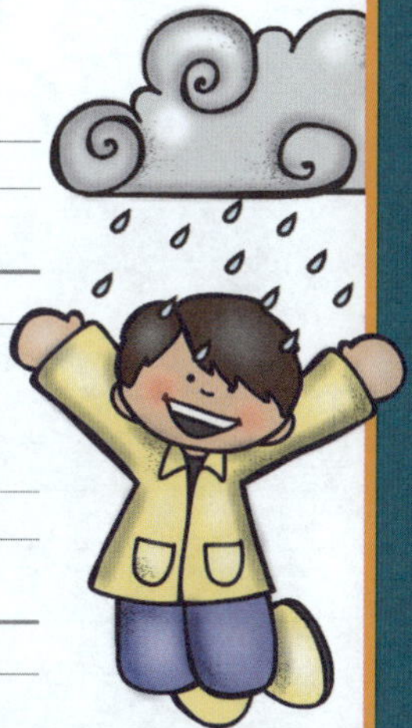

Wonderful! Take a sticker.

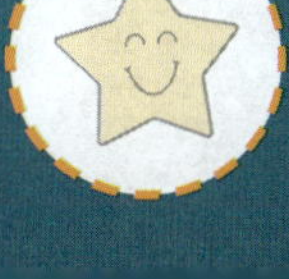

m and p

How It Works

Trace each letter. Start at the red dot. Then copy them.

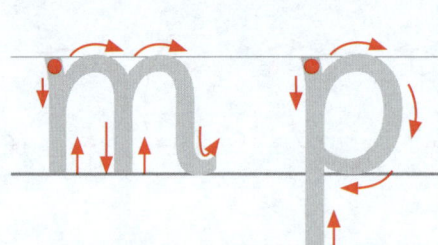

Now Try These

m m m

p p p

pose

camera

picture

frame

Smile! Take a sticker.

m and p

How It Works

Start at the red dot and trace each word. Then copy them.

Now Try These

my mum is super

my parents are fun

my uncle is popular

Marvellous! Go and grab a sticker.

d, g and q

How It Works

Starting at the red dot, trace each letter. Then copy them.

Now Try These

d d d

g g g

q q q

dragon

queen

guard

Nice one! Have a sticker.

d, g and q

How It Works

Trace the words and then copy them. Start each letter at the red dot.

Now Try These

quite a large dog

a queue of frogs

a squad of goats

You're doing great! Find a sticker.

h, b and k

How It Works

Trace each letter. Start at the red dot each time. Then copy them.

Now Try These

h h h

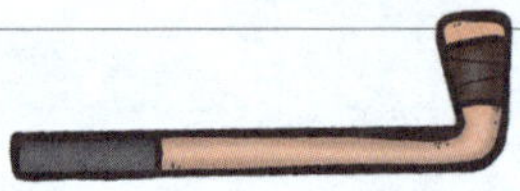

b b b

k k k

hit

bounce

kick

Amazing! Give yourself a sticker.

h, b and k

How It Works

Starting at the red dot, trace each word. Then copy them.

hot

Now Try These

it is hot at the beach

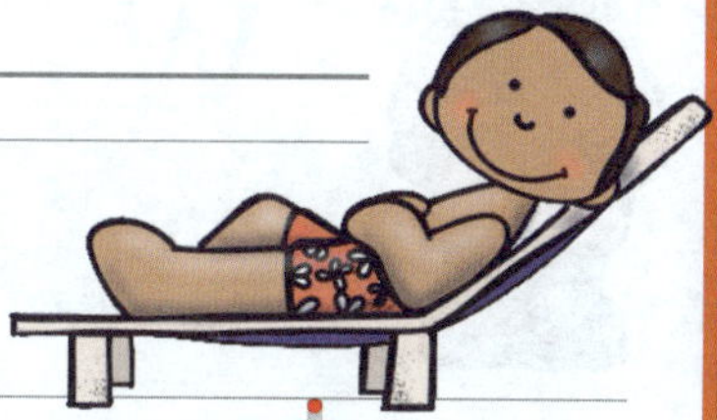

shells in her bucket

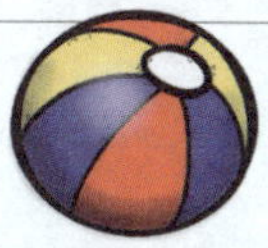

take a beach ball

You're the best! Stick on a sticker.

v, w, x and z

How It Works

Starting at the red dot each time, trace the letters and then copy them out.

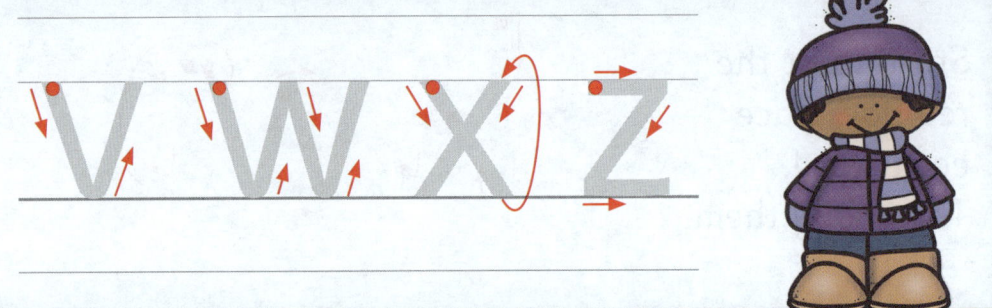

Now Try These

v   v   v

w   w   w

x   x   x

z   z   z

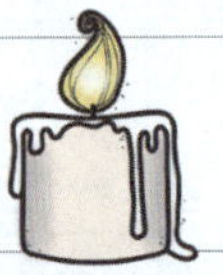

freeze   wax

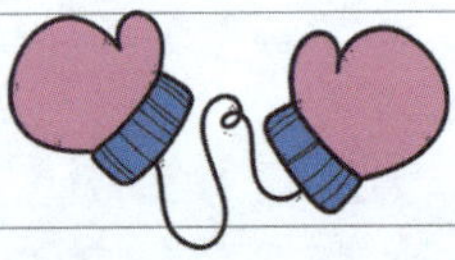

gloves

Brrrilliant! Take a sticker.

18

v, w, x and z

How It Works

Trace each word. Start at the red dot. Then copy them.

watch

Now Try These

we watch the fireworks

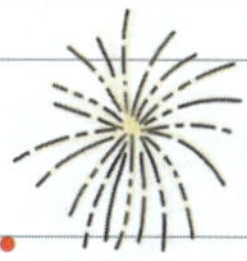

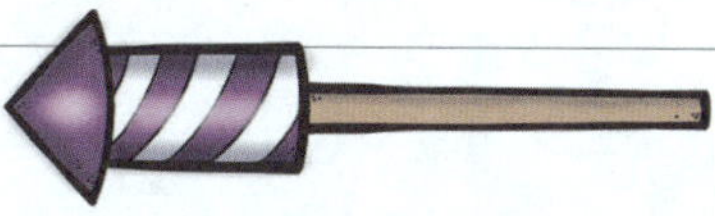

a very big explosion

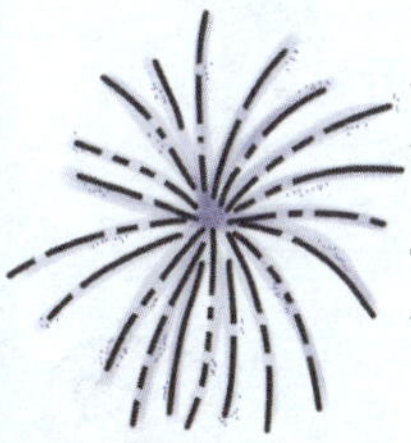

it was amazing

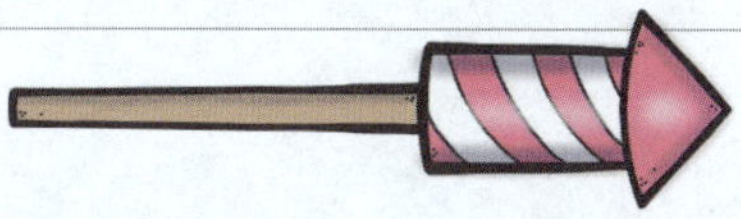

That was spectacular! Get a sticker.

19

Capital letters

How It Works

Start at the red dot and trace each letter. You will need to lift your pencil off the page for some of them.

Now Try These

A A B B

I I E E

Y Y G G

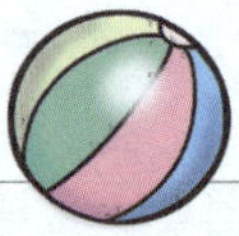

July

February

December

Sensational work! Pop on a sticker.

Capital letters

How It Works

Trace each word. Remember to start at the red dot. Then copy them.

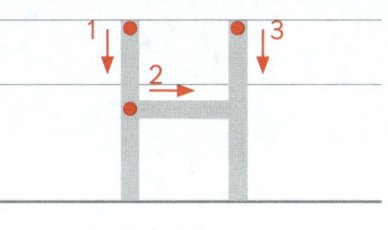

Now Try These

Helen

Kate

Raul

Nadia

Quinn

Liam

You did it! Go and find a sticker.

Numbers

How It Works

Trace each number. Then copy them. Start each number at the red dot. You will have to lift your pencil off for some of them.

Now Try These

0 0 0
1
2 2 2 
3 3 3   
4 4 4    
5 5 5

Not baaaa-d! Take a sticker.

Numbers

How It Works

Trace each number. Remember to start each number at the red dot. Then copy them.

Now Try These

6 6 6   7 7 7

8 8 8

9 9 9

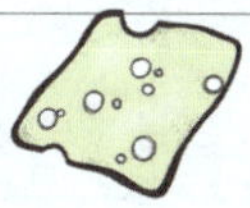

10 10 10

1 2 3 4 5

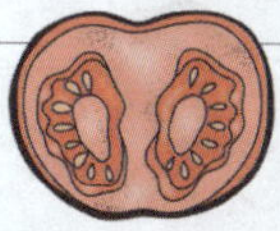

6 7 8 9 10

Yum! Give yourself a sticker.

A trip to the zoo

How It Works

Here is part of a letter. Trace the words and then copy them out. Don't forget the punctuation marks.

Now Try These

Friday 4th May

Dear Benjy,

Today I visited the zoo.

I saw a huge lion!

Roar-some job! Have a sticker.

A recipe for pancakes

How It Works

Tej and Lizzie are making pancakes. Here is their recipe. Trace the words and then copy them out.

Now Try These

In a big bowl, mix

75g of flour, 2 eggs

and some milk.

Cook in a wide pan.

That's pan-tastic! Find a sticker.

The Vikings

How It Works

Here are some facts about the Vikings. Trace the words and then copy them out.

Now Try These

The Vikings lived over

800 years ago.

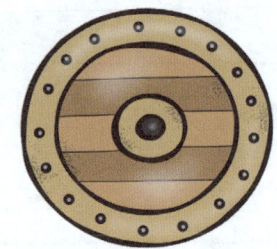

They built ships

called longboats.

You're doing great! Pick a sticker.

Jay's shop

How It Works

Here is some information about Jay's shop. Trace the words and then copy them out.

Now Try These

Jay owns a sweet shop.

Today he sold

36 marshmallows

and 9 chocolate bars.

Sweet! Give yourself a sticker.

Squid

How It Works

Here are some facts about a sea creature. Trace the words and then copy them out.

Now Try These

Squid live in seas and oceans.

Giant squid can be up to 13 metres long.

You're doing so well! Catch a sticker.

Hibba the detective

How It Works

Here is some information about Hibba. Trace the words and then copy them out.

Now Try These

Hibba is a detective.

She looks for clues

and solves mysteries

throughout the town.

You've cracked it! Can you uncover a sticker?

Perfect pastimes

Oops! Ava and her friends tried to write down their hobbies, but they got the words back-to-front. Can you help them? Work out each child's hobby and write it correctly on the lines in joined-up writing. Then use the stickers to fill in the things each child needs for their hobby.

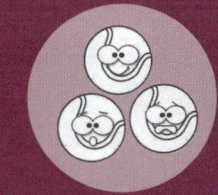

basketball

tennis

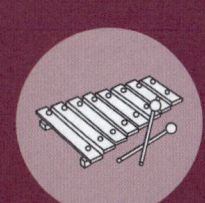

music

reading

skateboarding

Joining to small letters

How It Works

Are you ready for some joined-up writing? The first join is all about joining to small letters from the bottom. Practise it by tracing these pairs of letters, then copying them.

Now Try These

ar   ar   ar

up   up   up

ly   ly   ly

ni   ni   ni

mu   mu   mu

iv   iv   iv

You're flying now! Give yourself a sticker.

Joining to small letters

How It Works

These words all contain the first join. Trace each word and then copy it.

Now Try These

hump hump

cup cup

any any

mum mum

tiny tiny

lump lump

Out-sand-ing! Take a sticker.

33

Joining to e

How It Works

When you join from the bottom of a letter to an **e**, the **e** tilts slightly. Trace the letters and then copy them, starting at the red dot each time.

Now Try These

me   me   me

de   de   de

le   le   le

ce   ce   ce

mine   mine

ten   ten

Hip hip hooray! Grab a sticker.

34

Joining to e

How It Works

Practise joining to **e** from the bottom of a letter by tracing each word. Then copy them.

Now Try These

den den

lime lime

nine nine

tie tie

time time

deep deep

Brilliant! Stick on a sticker.

Joining small and tall letters

How It Works

The second join goes from the bottom of a small letter to a tall letter. To practise, trace and copy these pairs of letters.

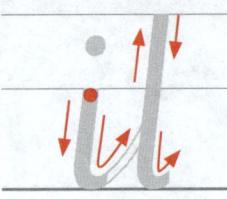

Now Try These

il il il

ab ab ab

if if if

ch ch ch

at at at

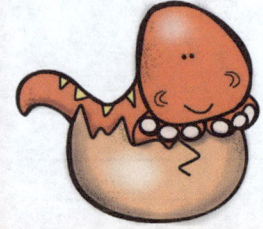

el el el

Amazing! Go and get a sticker.

Joining small and tall letters

How It Works

Trace these words and then copy them out. They all contain the second join.

Now Try These

climb   climb

helmet   helmet

like   like

hill   hill

club   club

cheer   cheer

You're reaching new heights! Find a sticker.

Joining small and tall letters

How It Works

Trace each sentence. Then copy them out. Start each word at the red dot. Remember that capital letters do not join to other letters.

Now Try These

I am the chief chef.

Will Sally chew it all?

We like the milk.

Delicious! Give yourself a sticker.

Joining to round letters

How It Works

The third join goes from the bottom of a letter to a round letter. You'll need to go back on yourself to write the second letter. Trace and copy these letter pairs to practise.

Now Try These

co   co   co

ha   ha   ha

ad   ad   ad

ng   ng   ng

dc   dc   dc

eq   eq   eq

You're making a splash! Have a sticker.

39

Joining to round letters

How It Works

These words all contain the third join. Trace them and then copy them.

Now Try These

act   act

dance   dance

lady   lady

man   man

child   child

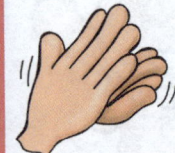

hand   hand

Amazing performance! Find a sticker.

Joining to round letters

How It Works

Start at the red dot and trace each sentence. Then copy it out.

Now Try These

Flo and Zac like tuna.

Milo made cake.

I need nice ham to eat.

Nice one! Stick on a sticker.

Joining to s

How It Works

When you write the third join to an **s**, the join is the same but slightly longer. The **s** also tilts a little. Trace and copy the letters and words below.

Now Try These

as   as   as

ds   ds   ds

ns   ns   ns

thinks   thinks

tails   tails

meals   meals

Excellent work! Take a sticker.

Joining from the top

How It Works

The fourth join goes from the top of one letter to the top of the next. Practise it by tracing and copying these letters. Be careful, the join is a slightly different shape when you're joining to **e**.

Now Try These

or   or   or

vy   vy   vy

wi   wi   wi

rn   rn   rn

ve   ve   ve

re   re   re

That was llamazing! Pop on a sticker.

Joining from the top

How It Works

Trace and then copy these words that all contain the fourth join. Remember that the join to **e** is a slightly different shape.

Now Try These

win   win

victory   victory

run   run

hop   hop

move   move

hurry   hurry

You're a winner! Pop a sticker on.

Joining from the top

How It Works

These sentences all contain the fourth join. Trace and copy each of them.

Now Try These

Your trek will take one hour.

Continue down the river.

It is very windy out here.

You did it! Find a sticker.

45

Joining from f

How It Works

To do the fourth join from an **f**, you need to lift your pencil off the page. Trace and copy the letters below to practise.

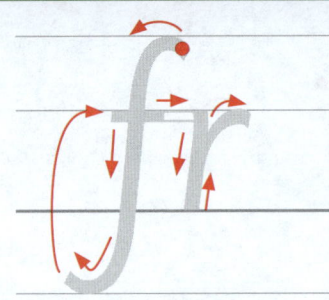

Now Try These

fr   fr   fr

fu   fu   fu

fe   fe   fe

five   five

furry   furry

comfy   comfy

Paws-itively perfect! Have a sticker.

More joining from the top

How It Works

The fifth join connects the top of a small letter to the middle of a tall letter. To practise, trace and copy these pairs of letters.

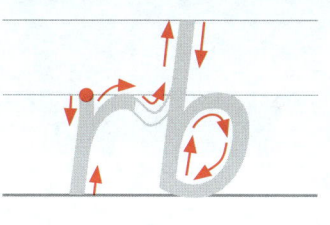

Now Try These

rb rb rb

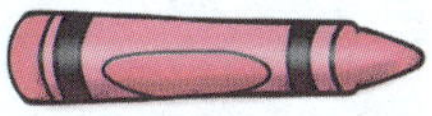

ot ot ot

wl wl wl

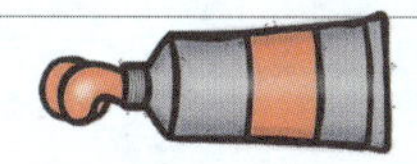

rk rk rk

of of of

wh wh wh

Outstanding work! Give yourself a sticker.

More joining from the top

How It Works

These words all contain the fifth join. Trace each word and then copy it out.

Now Try These

owl   owl

cold   cold

dark   dark

white   white

tart   tart

colour   colour

What a hoot! Stick on a sticker.

More joining from the top

How It Works

Trace and copy these sentences. They all contain the fifth join.

Now Try These

Rob has a violet turkey.

Molly has lots of moths.

Johnny loves turtles.

Wild! Take a sticker.

More joining from f

How It Works

When you write the fifth join from an **f**, you have to lift your pencil off the page. To practise, trace and copy these letters and words.

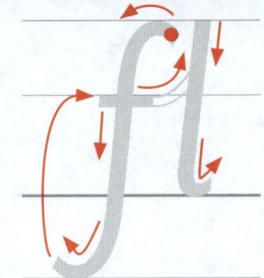

Now Try These

fl   fl   fl

ft   ft   ft

ff   ff   ff

flip   flip

lift   lift

cliff   cliff

That was snow much fun! Get a sticker.

More joining to round letters

How It Works

The sixth join goes from the top of a letter to a round letter. You have to go back on yourself when you write the second letter. Trace and copy these letters to practise.

Now Try These

rg   rg   rg

wd   wd   wd

oc   oc   oc

vo   vo   vo

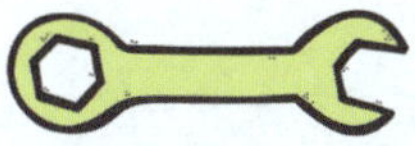

fa   fa   fa

rs   rs   rs

You're on a roll! Give yourself a sticker.

51

More joining to round letters

How It Works

All of these words contain the sixth join. Trace each word and then copy it out.

Now Try These

water   water

rock   rock

wave   wave

crab   crab

rod   rod

ocean   ocean

You rock! Give yourself a sticker.

More joining to round letters

How It Works

Trace and then copy these sentences that contain the sixth join.

Now Try These

Noah travels to the Moon.

The rocket was far away.

I want to walk on Mars.

Blast off! Grab a sticker.

Break letters

How It Works

Break letters don't join to the next letter. The break letters are **b**, **g**, **j**, **p**, **q**, **s**, **x**, **y** and **z**. Trace and copy these words that start with a break letter.

Now Try These

boy   boy

girl   girl

jump   jump

boots   boots

yellow   yellow

saddle   saddle

Yee-ha! Get yourself a sticker.

Break letters

How It Works

Trace and copy these words with break letters in the middle. Remember that you don't join to or from **x** and **z**.

Now Try These

hops   hops

rabbit   rabbit

apple   apple

fuzzy   fuzzy

unique   unique

excited   excited

Brilliant job! Stick on a sticker.

55

Break letters

How It Works

Trace and then copy these sentences that contain break letters.

Now Try These

Tulips grow in spring.

Abi enjoys planting seeds.

The garden looks amazing!

Your handwriting is blooming! Grab a sticker.

The school assembly

How It Works

James and his friends are performing in a school assembly. Trace these sentences about the assembly and then copy them.

Now Try These

James plays the flute.

Sarah is on the piano.

Monique sings a solo.

Baxter performs last.

Beautiful! Find yourself a sticker.

The friendly monster

How It Works

This poem is about a monster. Trace each line of the poem and then copy it out below.

Now Try These

The monster under my bed

Is not scary to me.

He is furry and purple

And as kind as can be!

Terrific work! Go take a sticker.

Ancient Egypt

How It Works

Here are some facts about the Ancient Egyptians. Trace the words and then copy them out.

Now Try These

The Ancient Egyptians lived

thousands of years ago.

They created mummies

and built pyramids.

Excellent! Stick a sticker on here.

Under construction

How It Works

Bibek's mum works on a building site. Trace these sentences about her job and then copy them out.

Now Try These

I always wear my hard

hat and an orange jacket.

Building walls is fun!

I really love my job.

Nailed it! Take a sticker.

A trip to the post office

How It Works

Here are some directions to the post office. Help Evie get there by tracing and copying each sentence.

Now Try These

Go straight on for 5 minutes.

Turn left at the school.

After 2 miles, turn right.

Arrive at the post office.

You made it! Get yourself a sticker.

The potion

How It Works

Read these sentences about a witch and her cat. Trace and then copy each line.

Now Try These

The witch stirred her potion.

It bubbled and fizzed.

Her cat stuck out a paw

and spilled it on the floor!

Wicked job! Grab a sticker.

Give yourself a star when you've finished an activity.

Use these stickers on the puzzle in the middle of the book.